SUCCESS NUGGET SERIES

VOL 1

MAXIMIZING
The Power Of
PURPOSE

A must-read for every student who desires success in his/her studies

SAMUEL O. OLULANA

MAXIMIZING THE POWER OF PURPOSE

Copyright [c] 2004 by:
SAMUEL O. OLULANA
Enlarged edition 2012
ISBN 978-978-50662-3-4
Reprinted 2017

Published in Nigeria by:
Treasured Word Publishing House

All Rights Reserved
Before any portion of this book can be used, written permission must be secured from the author or publisher, except for brief excerpt in magazine, articles, reviews etc.

All Scripture quotations, unless otherwise indicated are from the NEW KING JAMES VERSION of the Bible.

For Enquiries Write:
Treasured Word Publishing House
P. O .BOX 7035 Sapon,
Abeokuta, Ogun State. Nigeria.

Tel: [+234] 803 563 2431, 807 342 3909,803 486 1172
E-mail: twph@gmail.com

This Book Is A
GIFT

To

From

On The Occasion Of

Date

Know ye not that they which run in a race run all, but one receiveth the prize? So run, that ye may obtain.
1 Corinthians 9:24

TABLE OF CONTENT

Introduction 9

Chapter One:
Understanding Purpose 19

Chapter Two:
Winning Through Purpose 37

Chapter Three:
Time Does Not Heal All Wounds 51

Chapter Four:
Practical Guides To Maximize Purpose 61

Chapter Five:
The Final Word 69

Check Your Foundation!

Your Foundation Determines Your Future

09

I THEREFORE SO RUN, NOT AS UNCERTAINLY; SO FIGHT I, NOT AS ONE THAT BEATETH THE AIR.
1Cor. 9:26 [KJV]

INTRODUCTION

It is a common saying that there can never be a smoke without fire. This statement put in another way simply means, any time you notice a smoke anywhere, it simply means that there is a fire burning somewhere.

This statement is not only the truth, but it also has a lot of lessons to teach every right thinking student as well as individuals, particularly when we talk about his / her

Introduction

Therefore the desire of every right thinking student at all levels of study and at every point in any given time should be, what must be done for him or her to succeed in his or her academic pursuit.

One un-contestable truth we can learn from the above statement is that, though success is good and it is the desire of every right thinking student, and every individual in his right mind, it is not cheap to get. Only the people, or rather the students, who are not just wishing to get it, but are ready to give it all that it will take to get it at any given time or level will eventually get it.

Mr "Success," I want you to know is like a crown, and it has no permanent friend, and no permanent enemy. It is always found anywhere it is welcomed.

chosen field of endeavour or pursuit in life.

Friend, if anybody anywhere tells you that a smoke can come forth without fire burning somewhere, then such a person must either be doing what I call an **"expensive joke" or deceiving himself, or he is out of his mind.** The absolute truth is: No fire, no smoke. Period.

> PLEASE UNDERSTAND THAT EVERY SUCCESS STORY THAT HAS EVER HAPPENED UNDER HEAVEN HAS A SECRET BEHIND IT, AND THIS INCLUDES ACADEMIC EXCELLENCE.

Beloved, success in your academic pursuit is very good. In fact success in any giving area of one's academic pursuit is the best thing that can ever happen to any student.

Maximizing The Power Of Purpose

Every student desires to wear the crown of success, but the truth is that not every student will eventually wear it. This is because the crown of success is the result which is always available to every individual student who is ready to carry the "cross that produces success" in his chosen career. Thus, it is a common saying that no cross, no crown.

Friend, if you are in the group of those 'useless students' who think that success in life as well as in academic pursuit is obtainable anyhow [i:e through luck, or unholy means], you must know from today that you are nobody other than a great joker. You are like someone chasing his own shadow. You are like someone on a mission that has no destination. You have just embarked on a project that has no end.

Introduction

The earlier you return from such a journey, the better it is for you, and for your overall success, particularly in your academic pursuit.

Please, give the following statement a good attention: ***success is a choice, and failure is also a choice.*** Whether you will succeed in your academic pursuit or not is only a product of the choice you make today either consciously or unconsciously.

Please understand that every success story that has ever happened under heaven has a secret behind it, and this includes academic excellence. Until you lay hold on this secret as far as your academic pursuit is concerned, you are a registered failure in the school you are presently.

The aim of this book therefore, is to show you one of these hidden, but wonder

Maximizing The Power Of Purpose

working "chemicals" when we talk about success in your academic work. This volume will show you, what a student with a PURPOSE will achieve.

We all know that purpose is the reason for doing what you do at any particular time. There is a reason why you are in school. If you can grab it, failure of any kind will be a thing of the past in your academic pursuit. And you will then begin to enjoy accelerated success in your studies.

Please read this book [***Neglected Secret for Academic Excellence Vol. 1***] and the other ones in the series with every carefulness, diligence, and also with the mind to make as many discoveries as possible from it, which will eventually transform into a strong decision within you to succeed.

Introduction

You will surely get to the top in life in Jesus' mighty name.

Watch Your Lifestyle!

If You Don't, Your Future Is At STAKE

BUT DANIEL PURPOSED IN HIS HEART THAT HE WOULD NOT DEFILE HIMSELF WITH THE PORTION OF THE KING'S DELICACIES, NOR WITH THE WINE WHICH HE DRANK; THEREFORE HE REQUESTED OF THE CHIEF OF THE EUNUCHS THAT HE MIGHT NOT DEFILE HIMSELF. Dan. 1:8

CHAPTER ONE

UNDERSTANDING WHY YOU ARE IN SCHOOL

Dear friend and student, each time you hear anyone talking or discussing about academic excellence, please know and understand that they are simply talking about you making tangible and touchable success in your academic pursuit.

By extension, we are also talking about the few disciplined individual boys and girls in our various institutions of learning who know the singular purpose of leaving their various parents' homes or their school hostels to their respective school classrooms every day to receive lectures.

I will like you to know that the greatest tragedy that has befallen many of the present day students scattered in our various primary, secondary, and tertiary

> **WHEN THE PURPOSE OF SOMETHING IS NOT KNOWN, THEN, ABUSE OF THAT THING IS INEVITABLE**

institutions of learning today is the fact that a great many of them have failed to realize that it is going to be practically impossible for any student to get good and outstanding success in his or her respective academic pursuit without his

Understanding Why You Are In School

or her readiness to pay the price that will make him or her to practically possess it.

Dear student, to have a good result in your academic pursuit, you must be ready to pay the necessary price for it. This is not negotiable. No matter who you are or who your parent is, you cannot avoid this truth.

One out of the many compulsory prices you must pay is that you must become purposeful in your academic pursuit. You must realize that there is a reason why you are in school at any particular point in time, and not at somewhere else. You must be bold and courageous enough to avoid every form of distraction in your academic pursuit that are contrary to the reason why your parents sent you to school.

Please, take your time and meditate on the

Maximizing The Power Of Purpose

following statement you are about to read. ***There is no way for you to achieve any good grade in your studies, if you fail to discover the purpose for your coming to school.*** This is because when the purpose of a thing is lost, abuse of the use of that thing is inevitable. ***When you don't know the purpose of being in the school, then you are bound to pursue another agenda which you must have created for yourself, [unconsciously], or which someone else has created for you with your permission or your carelessness.***

Dearly beloved student, in this book I will be sharing with you the secret of how you can secure a life-time of great benefits for yourself. These are benefits that will allow you not just to enjoy the joy of making

Understanding Why You Are In School

good grade in your studies but will also give you a place of recognition among your friends, loved ones, and your community as well as in your country of abode and beyond.

The secret I will be sharing with you in this book is what I call ***understanding the reason why you are in school***. This book, I want you to know, is out to show you how you can achieve the best from your academic pursuits through the effective use of the power of purpose. ***You have to be purposeful in whatever you do in order for you to fulfill your purpose in life, because, if you fail to know the reason why you are in school, you will end up doing something that is contrary to the reason of your being in school.***

Maximizing The Power Of Purpose

Dear student, if you can discover and utilize the power of purpose - which is one of the many needed catalysts for academic excellence, I can tell you with all assurance that your success in your academic pursuit is not negotiable.

Hear this: no teacher anywhere or in any

> **PURPOSE IS THE REASON WHY YOU DO WHAT YOU DO AT ANY POINT IN TIME.**

school under heaven has the power or the right to determine which student will pass well or fail woefully in any examination. The power or the right to make such a decision is the exclusive preserve of every student. It is the responsibility of every

Understanding Why You Are In School

student to determine what he or she will get from any examination, and this is why you see students of the same class who have received the same lectures getting different results in an examination.

I want you therefore, to please carefully read this book, and study it very diligently also, so that you can get the maximum benefit of its contents. This book is out to help you discover what purpose is, and how you can utilize purpose to your best advantage.

Please note that purpose or the reason why you anything is a very critical factor concerning any issue or area of your endeavour. It is the reason for your coming to the school to receive lectures every blessed day, and not being at another place, doing something else.

Please understand also that anything you do without knowing its purpose is surely

> **PLEASE UNDERSTAND ALSO THAT ANYTHING YOU DO WITHOUT KNOWING ITS PURPOSE IS SURELY GOING TO END UP AS A WASTED EFFORT.**

going to end up as a wasted effort. Why? It is simply because such efforts are like the case of someone chasing his own shadow; and you and I know that, no matter how fast you can run, you as a person will never be able to catch up with your own shadow, most importantly when it is standing in front of you.

It is a very sad thing that many students of this present age has failed to know the purpose of their coming to their various school classrooms on daily basis. Many have the wrong believe that what will be will be. This is not only a false belief but also a destroyer of great destinies. It is the devil's "gift" in disguise. If you receive this gift, you have traded your glorious future for nothing but great failure. Please be wise and act very wisely.

> **A PURPOSE DRIVEN MAN IS A MAN THAT CANNOT BE DISTRACTED**

Dear student, success in any area of life, I want you to know does not just happen to people, you will have to work hard for it if you truly want to become successful. You have to make it happen by following the golden rules of **_purposeful, hard and diligent study._** You have to learn how to burn the midnight candle instead of sleeping throughout the night like a man that is going no where in life.

In any school today, worldwide, you will always find two groups of students: those that are in the school to make it [pass] and those that are there in the school to fail. These two groups will always be found in any school irrespective of the teacher in charge of such etudents, the facilities available in such schools, or who the proprietor / proprietress of the school is.

Note this: No matter how hard any teacher tries to teach his / her students, whether such a student will succeed or not depends to a large extent on the impute of the student involved. There is a limit to the

Understanding Why You Are In School

extent any teacher or the parent can go to make a particular student attain good grades.

Listen, it is often said that you can force a horse to the river, but it is not possible for you to force the horse to drink from the river after you might have forced the horse to the river. This is a truth that is constant for students, teachers and parents.

Any parent can force his or her ward to the school. Others might struggle to enrol their children in the best school in town, but whether the student involved will succeed excellently or fail woefully, will be determined to a large extent by the disposition of such student to his or her studies. Every other efforts is only to aid and assist the student, they are not the major determinant; they are all good for anything; events that took place in my family shortly after the release of my result - particularly between me, my immediate senior brother and his wife - forced me to make some very drastic and decisive decisions. Neither my teacher nor my parents were involved. It was purely a purpose-driven decision, which was based on my determination to win in life, even against all the odds around me.

The first step I took was to go back and re-enrol for another West African Examination Council examination despite the fact that no one was available to sponsor my education.

Right from the point I re-enrolled for another West African Examination Council examination, I made up my mind to settle for nothing other than a very good result.

Understanding Why You Are In School

My purpose was to pass excellently and continue with my studies at the University no matter what happens. I was determined to sponsor my education, if no one would sponsor me.

One of the subjects which was a problem for me was Mathematics. Believe me, beloved, I was very poor in this particular subject and I hated it with passion, but I had a younger brother who happened to have a good grasp of this subject. What I did was to bury my pride, and beg him to teach me this subject and at the end of the day I had a C6 without any external help during the examination; no cheating, no "giraffe method" during the examination. This is what purpose will give you, if you will embrace it.

I purposed in my heart to pass without

Maximizing The Power Of Purpose

compliments to his or her imputes into his or her studies.

For instance, the teacher could spend the whole day explaining a single topic in a particular subject to a given set of students; their parents could decide to send them to the best school in the land and even get the best private teachers available for him or her. All these efforts from both the teachers and the parents are not enough to guarantee success for any student. If the student involved fail to study, he will still fail very woefully.

All the efforts from both the teachers and the parents can only help or influence success, they cannot produce it, except the student in question is determined and ready to pay the price of success, which is hard work, a very diligent study which is influenced by purpose.

Some years ago, I sat for the West African Examination Council [WAEC]. This was in the early 1980's. When the result was released I got credit in two subjects and a pass in three other subjects. What a terrible result! You know as well as I do that

> **A PURPOSEFUL MAN IS ALWAYS A GOAL GETTER, BECAUSE HE IS A FOCUSED MAN.**

this is not a good result at all. It can carry nobody to nowhere as far as admission into any higher institution of learning is concerned.

This result, apart from the fact that it is not

cheating in the examination hall and I followed my decision with hard study. I decided to do away with all friends who could distract my attention. I also refused to get engaged in anything that could hinder my concentration as far as my study was concerned, and at the end of the day, God crowned my efforts with great success.

Therefore, I make bold to say that if any student wants to succeed in his or her academic pursuit, there are certain things he or she must intentionally purpose to do and not to do. This is a must decision every student must be ready to make. Every serious student should know that without his or her readiness to do some things and refusing to do some other things, as and when necessary, he or she is only kidding

Understanding Why You Are In School

as far as success in his or academic pursuit is concerned.

One of the things which every serious minded student must not fail to know is his or her purpose of coming to the classroom every day. This is very important. Its importance to success is like the importance of blood to the body system. When the body of any man lacks blood, then death is inevitable for that man. As a student, you must be bold enough to ask yourself why you are in the school and not at the mechanic workshop somewhere, or at any other place doing some other things

Let me be very sincere with you; when any student loses focus of the purpose of his or her coming to school, he / she is destined to fail, no matter what the teachers and the parents do to help the student in question.

Maximizing The Power Of Purpose

A body without blood is a dead body, because life is missing. So also, any student that lacks purpose has lost focus, and surely he or she will end up a failure, because he or she has already lost the focus of where he or she is going in life. What a great tragedy of life! What a waste of precious time and money!

Check This Out!

You Are The Next On The Line For Celebration

45

I PRESS TOWARD THE MARK FOR THE PRIZE OF THE HIGH CALLING OF GOD IN CHRIST JESUS. *Phip. 3:14*

CHAPTER TWO

EXCELLENCE THROUGH PURPOSEFUL LIVING

I said in the preceding chapter that purpose is the reason for doing what you do at any point in time. For instance, to the student reading this book now, purpose as far as your academic pursuit is concerned is the reason why you leave your home, or your school hostel to the school classroom every day, and not going somewhere else to do something different.

Many students have lost focus on the

Maximizing The Power Of Purpose

purpose or the reason for their going to their various schools and that is why you see them engaging themselves in various anti-academic activities in their various schools today.

When some other students are in the classroom reading, and listening to lectures, these students are somewhere else doing something different. What a pity and a waste of time, energy and money; what a way to trade a great destiny for something that has nothing to offer them other than frustrations and failures in the near future; what a mad way to waste their parents' hard-earned resources.

Any student in any of the occultic group for instance, has lost the track of the purpose of his or her going to school. This is the absolute truth, because, that is not why he or she is in school. I pray that God will enhance your understanding of what I am sharing with you in this book in Jesus' name.

Dear student, there is no way you look at it or try to explain it, when what you are doing in school at any point in time is different from the reason why your parents send you to school, then, the purpose of your going to school is already defeated. Very shortly, you will regret actions, because you have missed the track that leads to success.

Also, any student who is engaged in fornication either with other students or with any of their teachers or lecturers has lost the way and the purpose of coming to school, because that is not what he or she has gone to do in the school, and that can never be the way to achieve good success. No. It is not.

Every student who is purpose-driven or conscious will do away with any habit, association and practices that are contrary to the purpose of his or her going to school. Every student should know that the purpose of being in school is to learn from his or her teacher, study what he or she has learned, sit for examination, and pass to show that he or she is ready for promotion.

Purpose, [in whatever you do] is like a fire locked up inside your bones looking desperately for expression. It has a way of taking any student to the top in any giving examination. You cannot be conscious of the reason for your going to the classroom every school day and still get yourself

Excellence Through Purposeful living

engaged in other things that are contrary to your pursuit [academic excellence]. It is not possible. "Mr purpose" in you will not allow it.

Anything contrary to excellence in your academic pursuit is like a weight put upon an athlete. You know he or she will not be able to run a successful race. The weight will surely weigh such an athlete down. This is exactly what any student will get when he or she gets engaged in anti - purpose activities while in school. Dear student, please wait at this point and ask yourself the following questions;

First, ask yourself, why am I in this school [put the name of your school therein]. In other words, ask yourself what have I come here [your school] to do?

Please be very sincere with yourself,

because the answer you give will have a profound impact upon your academic pursuit. It is capable of helping you to straighten up if you are already off course.

Ask yourself the second question [after you must have sincerely answered the first one], have I come here to play, or join the occultic group, or for sex, or to study and pass? If you can sincerely answer this second question, you are closer to fulfilling your destiny.

Then ask yourself the third question; The things I am doing now, will they help me to fail or to pass? Please be very sincere with yourself in answering these questions. Don't ever try to deceive yourself at all. Remember, this is your life we are talking about, it is not about another person's life, but your own life. If you make the stupid

Excellence Through Purposeful living

mistake of deceiving yourself now, you will surely cry for your act of deception of today in the nearest future.

I repeat, do remember that it is your own life that is at stake. So, if you play a "smart" game with your life now, you will only be doing yourself a great harm. You will be digging your own grave. May you be wise enough to appreciate the fact that you have your life to live, and that whatever you do with your life today is a seed you have planted, and you will surely reap the harvest very shortly.

These questions, when sincerely answered, will help you keep your purpose alive and intact. Even if you have lost it before, they will help you to re-discover the purpose for your coming to school and subsequently, they will give your academic pursuit real excellence-driven force.

Friend, you are meant to be great and that is why your parents sent you to school and your teachers spend their energy teaching you. Refuse therefore any form of side attractions that can stop or destroy the purpose of your going to school. This is my sincere and fatherly advice to you in particular.

You will not become a child of reproach to your parents in Jesus' name. Your star will shine and your fame shall surely spread forth like the morning star in Jesus' name.

Please try and get my other series on academic excellence. They will add something [at least] to your life which will fire you to the top excellently. You are meant for the top, refuse to die at the bottom.

Excellence Through Purposeful living

I love you and I remain your best friend. My prayer for you is that God will bless your efforts and crown it with success in Jesus' name. You will not fail again in your academic pursuit. The last failure you recorded will be the last one you will ever have in Jesus' name.

As you open to the next chapter, I pray that God will baptize you with great revelation for outstanding success in Jesus' precious name.

Repair The Damage!

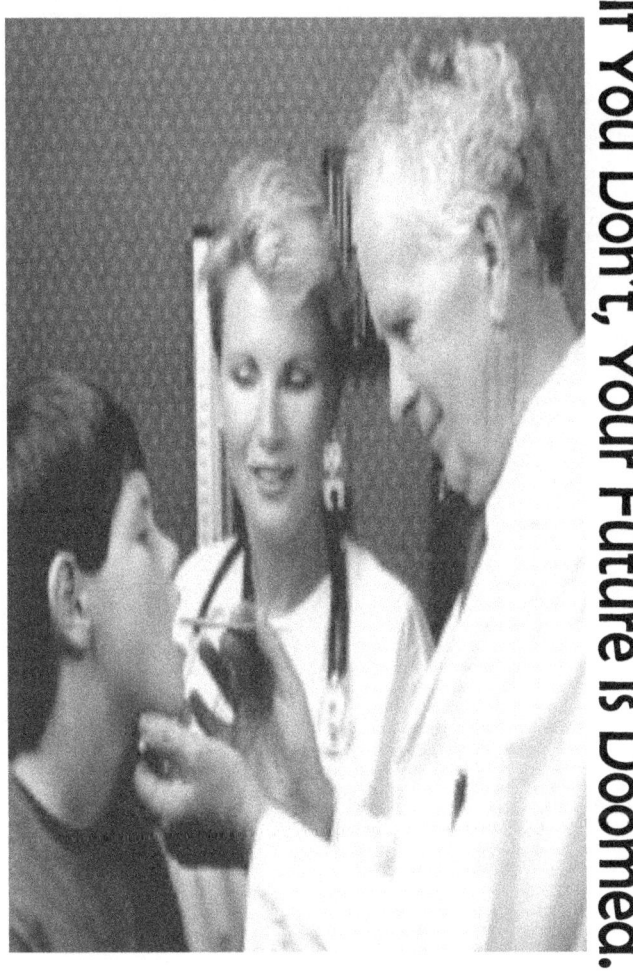

If You Don't, Your Future Is Doomed.

59

DO NOT REJOICE OVER ME, MY ENEMY; WHEN I FALL, I WILL ARISE; WHEN I SIT IN DARKNESS, THE LORD WILL BE A LIGHT TO ME.

Micah 7:8

CHAPTER THREE

TIME DOES NOT HEAL ALL WOUNDS

There is this evil saying among many of our people which has succeeded in destroying many glorious destinies. It goes thus: Time will heal the wound. This statement is not the total truth, and so, as far as I am concerned, it must not be relied upon by any serious-minded student or else, the end of such a student will be very disastrous.

Dear friend and student, the above statement is not only a false statement particularly when it is placed side by side with the academic pursuit of any student, it is also a word of deception from the pit of hell with the aim of destroying the life of the no purpose-driven students in their academic pursuit. What a great and cheap way through which many students have traded away their great and glorious destinies.

Take for example the case of a student who failed in his West African Examination Council examination some twenty years ago, if he refuses to re-write the said examination, up till the present year, will that long past years make him get a pass in that same examination? The answer is no. As long as he refuses to sit for that examination again, he remains a failure. Even if he waits for the next forty years, he will still be counted among the failures anytime and any day.

Dear student, even though this man has waited for twenty good years, those years

> **IF YOU FAIL TO TAKE CARE OF YOUR TODAY, THEN YOUR TOMORROW IS AT RISK.**

have no power to make him pass the examination. If he sincerely desires to have a pass in that examination, the only way for him to achieve that is for him to go back to school, re-enrol, and re-sit the said examination, and with better preparation he will make a good grade.

Listen to this my dear student: If you have failed in any examination, that is not your end. It is not an indication that you cannot make it again in life. The truth is that a hurdle has been given to you to cross. All you need to do is to accept your failure in good faith and gather yourselves together, prepare very well and put in for the examination again.

Dear reader, I want to sincerely encourage you to please be humble enough to know that your life will amount to absolute nothing in the near future if you fail to bury your pride now and do what is right and see that you do it at the right time. This may sound very hard, but it is the absolute truth.

I am a living witness to what I am sharing with you in this book. I was once a failure, but I braced up with the challenge of a failure by not allowing it to weigh me down. I gathered my books together again, read

Time Does Not Heal All Wounds

very well, avoided all distractions, and re-wrote my West African Examination Council Examination. When the result was released I was among the students who scored very good grades.

Dear student, I am begging you at this point , even in the name of your creator; the Almighty God, that you should not allow yourself to be defeated by the deception of the devil. Whatever is your present challenge as far as your education is concerned, please know that you still have the opportunity to make your tomorrow very colourful and great, by doing what you must do today.

Listen to me, opportunity will only make your life great if only it meets you prepared. When any opportunity comes your way and it meets you unprepared, it will surely fly over you. I know you won't like that to happen to you.

Who knows, in the nearest future, your community may be asked to present the next Commissioner for Education in your state, will you ever be considered for that post if you are not educated? It is not possible.

I have often hear people say that the cost of education is too expensive in this part of the world, but to such people my answer has always been, the cost of education has never been as expensive as the cost of ignorance.

Please pay the necessary price today so that your tomorrow will not end up in regret. I love you and pray for you that you will make it to the top of your career in life in Jesus name.

You Need Guidance!

Any Life That Is Not Guided Will Go Off Course.

I WILL INSTRUCT YOU AND TEACH YOU IN THE WAY YOU SHOULD GO; I WILL GUIDE YOU WITH MY EYE.

Psalms 32:8

CHAPTER FOUR

PRACTICAL GUIDES TO MAXIMIZE PURPOSE

In this chapter, I hope to give you by the grace of God, some very practical guides and Godly wisdom, which I know, and am fully convinced of. If you will be humbled enough to put them to practice, you will be able to secure your destiny from destruction, and end your academic career with a wonderful result.

Let me tell you something: there can never be a successful story without a secret behind it. If you can locate the secret behind any success, then, without fail you can duplicate that success at any point in time and at any place under heaven. Please, ponder over the following points very well.

WATCH THE FRIENDS YOU WILL WALK WITH

The first hint or wisdom that I want to share with you is that you should watch very carefully the association you keep, or will keep at any point in time. The Bible says: <u>he that walk with the wise shall be wise, but the companion of fools shall be destroyed</u>. A wise man has also said: <u>show me your friends and I will tell you who you are.</u>

Dear student, I want you to know that the friends you walk with can either affect your academic life positively or negatively. No matter how good you are, if you choose to keep company with rascals in your school, it is just a matter of time before you too will become a rascal. There is an adage that says: if a she-goat chooses to walk with a dog, very shortly, that she-goat will be eating faeces. Please be very watchful and act very carefully.

Hear me: friendship is suppose to be by choice and not by force. You have the liberty to choose who you will walk with and who you don't want to walk with. Do you know that there are many students from very good homes who have suddenly become a problem to their family because of the bad company they keep in school. I want you to please be very careful with the friends you associate with because directly or indirectly, they have some impacts they

Maximizing The Power Of Purpose

will make upon your life and by extension your academic career.

BE BOLD TO SAY NO TO IMMORAL ACTS

Another wisdom or practical guide that I want to share with you is that you must be very careful about what you do with your time and life. There are some activity that you should not involve yourself in as a student. Can I ask you a question? What are you doing with a boy-friend now as a female student, or what are you doing with a girl-friend now as a male student.? You don't need either a boy-friend or a girl friend now.

Practical Guides To Maximize Purpose

Listen to me my dear student; it is not a crime for you to have a student of the opposite sex as a friend, but it is totally bad for you to engage in sexual acts with a friend of the opposite sex as a student. That is not what you are in school to do.

Some of you female students usually have sex with your male teachers or lecturers in order that you may be given cheap marks. This is also very bad and contrary to the purpose of why you are in school.

There is time for everything. Please, wait for your time. That time will come, when you will have sex and become tired of it. Why are rushing into it now? Mind this evil act so that it does not destroy your academic career. If you don't contact AIDS, you may become pregnant in the process, and that will jeopardize your academic career. Do you want that? Please be very careful with the way you handle your life.

AVOID THE DEVIL'S BLESSINGS

Another wisdom I want to share with you is that you should be careful with the gifts that comes across your way. There are some gifts you must refuse to take as a female student from the opposite sex, and from your male teachers. They could turn out to be a trap for you. You have to be contented with whatever your parents could give to you, else you will find yourself entangled with the gift of the devil. When your male teacher entices you with "a questionable" gift you must be bold enough to say no, and thank you thank him in a very humble way, so as not to be labeled a rude student by the school authorities. Be wise and learn to act wisely.

HAVE A GUIDE SYSTEM IN PLACE

The last wisdom or practical guide I want to share with you in this volume is that you put in place a check and balance system that will guide all that you will do as a student, so as not to allow carelessness to rob you of your desired academic excellence. My dear friend, please anything you cannot do in the open know that it is evil, so, keep away from it permanently.

No student is bold enough to smoke cigarette in the school premises because if he or she is seen doing that, he or she may be expelled from school. No student can openly say he or she is a member of a secret cult. So, why are you involved in it?

Dear student, any time you are about to do anything and you don't have the boldness to do it in the open just conclude that it is evil and run away from it. This way you will save yourself a lot of pains and regrets.

CHAPTER FIVE

THE FINAL WORD OF ADVISE

Having come this far, I am sure you must have learnt one or two lessons, which I strongly believe will go a long way to help you achieve excellence in your academic career if you will be diligent enough to put those things you have learnt to practice.

Let me tell you this: it is one thing for you to discover the truth, yet, it is another thing entirely for you to put the discovered truth into practice. Until you practice the discovered truth, it is of no relevance to your life.

My final word of advice to you is that you must not allow any temporary pleasure to rob you of your glorious future no matter how juicy it looks like. You are in the school to learn and that is what you must engage yourself doing. Never allow anything that is contrary to this, take you away from your primary purpose of coming to school. This is very important, and it can never be overemphasised.

Your parents have done their best by sending you to school. You should be wise and diligent enough to see that you make them happy; so that they will not have any occasion to regret spending the money they have spent on your education. Don't ever give the room for them to regret sending

The Final Word Of Advice

you to school at any point in time. This is one of the things you owe them, and you have no choice other than to give it to them.

You will not fail in Jesus' name. The last failure you had before is the last one you would ever have in Jesus' name. Please, have this in mind; if anyone will fail in life, that person must definitely not be you. My God will surely help you and see you through victoriously in Jesus mighty name.

I hope to hear very good and outstanding testimonies from you very soon, by the grace of God, in Jesus' name.

I love you and wish you well in life.

Please do your best to see that you get the other series of NEGLECTED SECRET FOR ACADEMIC EXCELLENCE. One thing I can assure you is that each one of them has something good to add to your life.

You are welcome to a world of unending opportunities and success in Jesus' name.

VERY PRECIOUS INFORMATION

Friend, have you ever considered giving your life to the Lord Jesus as something of a very great importance, and which you must do with much urgency? If you have not done it before, I strongly advise that you do it **TODAY,** because another day may be too late.

Please, understand this: without Jesus Christ as the Lord over your life, your life is not only useless, it is also at a great risk. Any life without Christ is also faced with many crises.

Jesus Christ is calling you today, please don't refuse His call of love, neither harden your heart to His outstretched arm of grace towards you.

God will bless you richly as you yield to His glorious call to you today in Jesus name.

You are welcome into His glorious and life-changing kingdom.

For More Spiritual Help Write To:
P.O. Box 7035, Sapon Abeokuta
Ogun State, Nigeria.

E-mail: twph2013@gmail.com
Phone: 0813 666 2194, 0802 706 5871

What This Ministry Is All About

The activities of Samuel Olulana Ministries includes:

1. **Radio-** The radio broadcast, "Wisdom Impact", is reaching thousand of lives across the nations of the world.

2. **Television-** Overcomers hour, an internationally syndicated weekly programme features teachings on God's principles for living an overcomer's life.

3. **WLBI-** The ministerial training arm through which those who are in the ministry, and those preparing for ministry is trained for effective ministry work.

4. **Missions-** The ministry involved in serious mission project across the nations of the world.

5. **Literature-** Best-selling books and magazines through which the wisdom of and power of God are proclaimed.

6. **Crusades/Seminars-** Multitudes are ministered to at crusades and seminars across the globe, as Samuel Olulana declares the life-changing principles of God.

Other Books
By
Samuel O. Olulana

1. Creating Generational Wealth
2. Living In Dominion
3. Maximizing The Power Of Purpose
4. Turning Your Problem Into Testimonies
5. Understanding The Secret Of Victorious Living
6. Benefits Of Walking In Obedience
7. The Forsaken Truth
8. You shall Not Be Barren
9. Walking In The Miraculous
10. Enjoying Financial Dominion
11. Benefits Of Living Your Life On Purpose
12. Guide To Effective Prayer
13. You Have No Excuse To Fail
14. overcoming the challenges Of Life
15. How To Overcome Your Struggles
16. Wisdom For Uncommon Success
17. Enjoying The Unlimited Power Of The Unlimited
18. Wisdom For Daily Living

Get Your Copies Of:
Rev. OLULANA SAMUEL

LIFE-TRANSFORMING BOOKS & CD'S

These books and Cd's will open your mind to

KEYS TO GREATNESS IN LIFE

Available in many Christian bookshops across the nation

Or Call: 0813 666 2194;
 0813 665 9832
Or Visit: www.treasuredword.net

You will be glad you did.

For prayer, counseling, and spiritual help, call:
[+234] 803 563 2431; 703 155 0210

SEND YOUR PRAYER REQUESTS THROUGH THIS PAGE:
Please pray along with me on the following issues:

Please send this subscription / prayer sheet to:

SAMUEL OLULANA MINISTRIES INTERNATIONAL
P. O. BOX 7035, SAPON, ABEOKUTA, OGUN STATE, NIGERIA.

www.ingramcontent.com/pod-product-compliance
Lightning Source LLC
Chambersburg PA
CBHW031410040426
42444CB00005B/506